TEN MODERN
EVANGELISM
MYTHS

TEN MODERN
EVANGELISM
MYTHS
A Biblical Corrective

RYAN DENTON

Reformation Heritage Books
Grand Rapids, Michigan

Ten Modern Evangelism Myths
© 2021 by Ryan Denton

Reformation Heritage Books
3070 29th St. SE
Grand Rapids, MI 49512
616-977-0889
orders@heritagebooks.org
www.heritagebooks.org

Printed in the United States of America
21 22 23 24 25 26/10 9 8 7 6 5 4 3 2 1

Library of Congress Cataloging-in-Publication Data

Names: Denton, Ryan, author.
Title: Ten modern evangelism myths : a biblical corrective / Ryan Denton.
Description: Grand Rapids, Michigan : Reformation Heritage Books, [2021] | Includes bibliographical references.
Identifiers: LCCN 2020058372 (print) | LCCN 2020058373 (ebook) | ISBN 9781601788443 (paperback) | ISBN 9781601788450 (epub)
Subjects: LCSH: Evangelistic work.
Classification: LCC BV3790 .D4762 2021 (print) | LCC BV3790 (ebook) | DDC 269/.2—dc23
LC record available at https://lccn.loc.gov/2020058372
LC ebook record available at https://lccn.loc.gov/2020058373

For additional Reformed literature, request a free book list from Reformation Heritage Books at the above regular or email address.

For James

Contents

Foreword

The *Merriam-Webster* dictionary defines a *myth* as "an unfounded or false notion."[1] Myths abound in our day, but perhaps they are most tragic when they inform our evangelism. Evangelism, or the preaching of the good news of Christ to the lost, should be the desire of everyone Jesus has saved. Sadly, this is not always the case. In fact, recent statistics tell us that many people in North American churches are apathetic toward evangelism.

Why is this? Countless answers could be given, but perhaps foundationally the reason is that the church is weighed down with many misconceptions concerning the message, meaning, motive, and manner of evangelism. Oftentimes congregations do not have a solid starting point in this regard and thus are slow to make Christ's last Great Commission their first great concern (Matt. 28:18–20).

This is why I am thankful for this new work by Ryan Denton, *Ten Modern Evangelism Myths: A Biblical Corrective.* Contained in this helpful treatment

---

1. *Merriam-Webster*, s.v. "myth," https://www.merriam-webster.com/dictionary/myth.

are powerful scriptural arguments that dismantle prevalent mistaken beliefs regarding evangelism and recover sound foundations for it. With ten great cannons, Ryan blasts away many common rationalizations for not obeying the Lord's commission, leaving the Christian with no other godly choice than to follow the example of the early church in going "every where preaching the word" (Acts 8:4).

Throughout the centuries God has used works like this to stir up His people to great gospel endeavors. Think, for example, of Andrew Fuller's *The Gospel Worthy of All Acceptation*, which greatly impacted the life of William Carey, "the father of modern missions," motivating him to go to India to proclaim Jesus to the masses.[2] With such writing, God shows the saints that "always and everywhere the servants of Christ are under order to evangelize."[3]

My prayer is that God will use this well-written, well-balanced primer to this glorious end. I hope it will be used to dispel the many unbiblical ideas that the contemporary church often holds toward evangelism, so that we, by the power of the Holy Spirit, will confidently and collectively go and win souls for Christ (1 Cor. 9:19–23).

—Pastor Rob Ventura

---

2. A few years later, Carey published his monumental missionary manifesto titled *An Enquiry into the Obligations of Christians to Use Means for the Conversion of the Heathens*.

3. J. I. Packer, quoted in John Blanchard, comp., *The Complete Gathered Gold* (Darlington, England: Evangelical Press, 2006), 180.

Preface

The following is a compilation of the most popular misconceptions about modern evangelism, followed by a palatable and easy-to-read response through the lens of Reformed theology. This book is meant to be a manual for pastors, seminarians, lay Christians, missionaries, and anyone else who desires to have better insight into biblical evangelism, especially in contrast to approaches that are more gimmick-based and anthropocentric.

We are living in a time when a small revival of Reformed theology is shaking many homes and churches throughout the world. Many good sermons are being preached. Many good conferences are being held. Many good books are being written and read. But one area still lagging in Reformed theology is evangelism. Material on Reformed evangelism pales in comparison to the synergistic writings still popular today. This book is an attempt to help fill that void.

I have intentionally selected only ten evangelism myths to address since many more myths and problems are tackled under each heading. These ten myths seem to be the most pressing and foundational given our current context. Commenting on the relationship between the historic Reformed faith and evangelism, Joel Beeke notes, "The heroes of Reformed piety were often imbued with a missionary spirit, praying, sending, going—and suffering."[1] It is time we return to such a missionary spirit. It is my prayer that this short book will help better equip us to bring the gospel to the lost and to understand the importance of doing so in the right way. Some of the content in this book was developed from *Even if None: Reclaiming Biblical Evangelism.*[2] The permission to reprint these sections is acknowledged with appreciation.

---

1. Joel Beeke, *Reformed Preaching: Proclaiming God's Word from the Heart of the Preacher to the Heart of His People* (Wheaton, Ill.: Crossway, 2018), 74.

2. Ryan Denton, *Even if None: Reclaiming Biblical Evangelism* (San Francisco, Calif.: First Love Publications, 2019).

MYTH 1

Theology Doesn't Matter When Evangelizing

Is theology important when it comes to evangelizing the lost? Can't we just tell people about Jesus and not worry about stuff like doctrine? Many people in our day look at theology as impractical or superfluous when it comes to sharing the gospel. As we will see, such a perspective is woefully naive and has done much damage to the church. Like all other areas of Christian living, theology is critical when it comes to how we go about evangelism.

When Christians think or speak about God, man, the gospel, the purpose of the cross, the goal of evangelism, or how to live a Christian life, they are "doing" theology. Theology simply means the study of God. But not everyone's theology is correct, of course. One person thinks humans are unable to seek God because of the depravity of their faculties, including the mind. Another person believes humans, though sinful, are capable of seeking God through the use of a will that is neutral or indifferent to choose either good or evil. Such persons have entirely different views of God and man. Hence, their approach to evangelism and the message they communicate to unbelievers will be utterly different.

I am discussing the difference between Reformed and synergistic soteriology as it relates to evangelism. *Synergism* means both the divine and human wills must cooperate with each other if a person is to be saved, as opposed to *monergism*, which is the stance held by Reformed theology and means that God saves an individual according to His will alone, although God uses means to accomplish that end. The Bible is unapologetically monergistic, not synergistic. It teaches the doctrine of total or pervasive depravity. Every part of man has been tainted by sin, including his mind, will, emotions, and body (Gen. 6:5–6; Pss. 51:5; 58:3; Jer. 17:9; Rom. 3:9–18; Eph. 2:1–3). The Bible also teaches the total inability of man to act in a way distinct from his nature, and in the case of fallen man, his corruption. "Can the Ethiopian change his skin, or the leopard his spots? then may ye also do good, that are accustomed to do evil" (Jer. 13:23). Fallen man will always act in accordance with his fallen nature, which has no desire for God or the things of God.

This is why the Bible teaches "salvation belongeth unto the LORD" (Ps. 3:8; see also Jonah 2:9); salvation is the result of divine election from before the foundation of the world, without any foreseen merit in the one elected. Apart from God's saving grace, founded on His unconditional election, men will never choose to follow Christ. Jesus told us "a man can receive nothing, except it be given him from heaven" (John 3:27), which includes faith. God's grace is the only hope man has to be saved and, consequently, regarding evangelism, is the only hope we have when sharing the gospel. God must "rend the heavens" and "come down" (Isa. 64:1).

The person who holds to Reformed soteriology will be protected from two mindsets that the synergistic Christian often falls prey to. This is not to say the Reformed Christian will always be free from such dangers, but it is to say that, if consistent, it won't be as big of a threat. The first danger is discouragement, and with discouragement comes the tendency to use pragmatism and gimmicks in evangelism. The person who holds to Reformed soteriology believes God alone grants regeneration to the unbeliever and that the method God has given us for this purpose is the gospel. If people aren't being saved, the Reformed Christian won't resort to trickery or a watered-down message since it wouldn't help anyway. Nor will the Reformed Christian be discouraged, since conversion is God's work, not ours.

But the synergist, not seeing anyone saved through simple gospel proclamation, will still feel pressure to get the person converted. He must now resort to something else. At the very least he is going to become discouraged and put the blame on himself for not seeing others saved. Eventually he may become reluctant to evangelize at all, seeing how hard it is to get someone converted. This isn't to say the Christian should be unconcerned about the souls of men or how to best communicate the gospel, but the temptation to water down the message or become discouraged in the work of evangelism won't be nearly as strong.

Perhaps more dangerous, however, is the second difference that results from contrasting views of soteriology. If the Reformed Christian sees someone saved through his gospel efforts, he knows it was God alone who did it, not the one being witnessed to or the one witnessing. It wasn't his speech, his holy life, his wisdom, or anything else—it was God who had mercy (Rom. 9:16). On the contrary, the synergist must to some extent believe it was the person's decision or belief that saved him, not God's unconditional election. God made the person savable, but the person took the initiative to do the rest upon hearing the gospel. Such a mindset leads to pride in the one converted, since he's the one who believed, and pride in the one sharing the gospel, since he did so in such a way that the unbeliever accepted it.

God's unconditional election should be a great comfort to the Christian since it is not up to him to save sinners. The Christian does not need to rely on props or tricks when it comes to evangelism since "the natural man receiveth not the things of the Spirit of God: for they are foolishness unto him: neither can he know them, because they are spiritually discerned" (1 Cor. 2:14). Since God is sovereign in salvation and man is incapable of being born again apart from God's regenerating grace, the Christian can go out in total dependence on God. He will be liberated from the burden of "saying the right thing" or the fear of "saying the wrong thing." He cannot push people further away from God. People whose minds are set on the flesh are hostile to God (Rom. 8:7) and can't be pushed any further away from God than they already are.

Belief in God's unconditional election should also keep the Christian humble when evangelizing. It will never be his cleverness of speech or worldly wisdom that saves or attracts sinners to Jesus Christ (1 Cor. 1:17). Such a view will lessen the temptation of thinking the Christian has anything to do with someone's salvation, apart from sharing the gospel with them. The Christian will recall he is preaching to dry bones and that "the wicked, through the pride of his countenance, will not seek after God: God is not in all his thoughts" (Ps. 10:4). Without this understanding the Christian will try to entice the person's emotions in unbiblical ways. He will attempt to speak cleverly or trick an unbeliever in order to draw him to Christ, which is the opposite of Paul, who was unskilled as a speaker (2 Cor. 11:6).

A synergistic position detracts from the glory of God and leads to pride and false conversions. A synergist is always obligated to do all he can to manipulate the will of man into "choosing" God. This kind of evangelism will attempt to attract men with ritzy methods or eloquent and soft-peddled attractions, not the gospel. The notion of libertarian free will as it pertains to salvation is essentially in the same family as the Roman Catholic works-based system. It claims Christ has done His part, now you must do yours. Christ did a little, now you do a little. But if a person has to choose Christ in order to be saved, what does choosing entail? Walking an aisle? Saying a prayer? Raising a hand? Getting baptized? Anything the synergist puts forward will by default make it works-based.[1]

The Bible shows men are saved because God gives them a new heart (Ezek. 36:26), and when He does so, men repent and believe the gospel. God raises the spiritually dead to life. God loosens the shackles of sin. The only choice when it comes to salvation is God's, and rightly so. Christ prayed, "Thy will be done" (Matt. 6:10), not man's, because man's will is undone. This is why theology is so important when

---

1. The author does not mean to suggest all Arminians are lost or believe in the same "gospel" as the Roman Catholics. Much of this paragraph has been developed from a book coauthored by myself and Scott Smith, *A Certain Sound: A Primer on Open Air Preaching* (Grand Rapids: Reformation Heritage Books, 2019).

evangelizing. Without a right belief regarding God, man, the atonement, and other doctrines of Scripture, our approach to the lost will be unbiblical, as has been the case far too often in the history of the modern church.

Reflection Questions

1. What experiences have you had in evangelism that demonstrate how much theology matters?

2. Can someone who is theologically synergistic evangelize with a monergistic gospel, even if they don't know they are doing it? What about the opposite?

3. How does monergistic theology keep a person encouraged when evangelizing? Have you experienced this in your own life?

The Gospel Isn't Enough When Evangelizing

What happens if the people we evangelize don't get converted? Every Christian would admit the gospel is important, but is it ever okay to try something different, especially if we are not seeing a "positive" response? Hasn't God given us the right to be creative since He's the one who made us that way? Do the ends ever justify the means, supposing we see a lot of fruit from some other method? Are words always necessary? Can the gospel be communicated without them?

When Christians speak about the Bible, they are likely to agree it is infallible, inerrant, and hopefully even sufficient. But many Christians are more apt to believe that what the Scriptures say about evangelism and the gospel is not sufficient. Some are inclined to think our culture is much different from the early church's, and thus we must come up with other approaches if the lost are to be saved. Others believe we have a certain liberty to do things in ways that God hasn't necessarily prescribed—including evangelizing. But is it true that the Scriptures, or in this case the gospel, aren't enough when it comes to evangelism?

Before proceeding, we need to clarify what we mean by "the gospel." The word *gospel* is used here to include not only good news about Jesus but also the bad news, along with counting the cost of following Him. It is not good news unless the reality of a person's sin and the righteous judgement of God have been realized or at least explained. Also included in the gospel will be a clear call to repent and believe in Christ and an explanation of what it means to count the cost or to be a follower of Christ. This is not to assume every evangelism encounter will always have the same approach regarding these points. Each encounter will be different, but each of these topics requires an explanation in order to qualify as sharing the gospel.

The gospel is "the power of God unto salvation to every one that believeth" (Rom. 1:16). Will Metzger describes the gospel as "a word message announcing good news. The key Greek words connected to gospel refer to communication by words, talk, speech."[1] He also notes that "verbal communication [of the gospel] was the means by which the gospel spread."[2]

---

1. Will Metzger, *Tell the Truth* (Downers Grove, Ill.: Inter-Varsity Press, 1981), 32.

2. Metzger, *Tell the Truth*, 32.

This is why any approach to evangelism that makes the gospel secondary is unbiblical. "The key to biblical evangelism is not strategy or technique. It is not primarily about style, methodology, or programs and pragmatics. The first and preeminent concern in all our evangelistic efforts must be the gospel."[3]

When it comes to evangelism, this method of hearing the gospel is found throughout the Scriptures. Writing to the Romans, Paul says, "So then faith cometh by hearing, and hearing by the word of God" (Rom. 10:17). When writing to the Thessalonians he says, "For this cause also thank we God without ceasing, because, when ye received the word of God which ye heard of us, ye received it not as the word of men, but as it is in truth, the word of God, which effectually worketh also in you that believe" (1 Thess. 2:13). And again, when writing to the Galatians, Paul says, "Received ye the Spirit by the works of the law, or by the hearing of faith?" (Gal. 3:2). To the Ephesians he says, "In whom ye also trusted, after that ye heard the word of truth, the gospel of your salvation" (Eph. 1:13). This is where biblical evangelism comes in: "How then shall they call on him in whom they have not believed? and

---

3. John MacArthur and Jesse Johnson, "Rediscovering Biblical Evangelism," in *Evangelism* (Nashville, Tenn.: Thomas Nelson, 2011), viii–ix.

how shall they believe in him of whom they have not heard? and how shall they hear without a preacher?" (Rom. 10:14). Similarly, the following Greek verbs are used in the Acts of the Apostles to describe the work of evangelism: to testify (2:40), to proclaim and to teach (4:2), to preach the gospel (5:42), to herald (8:5), to confound (9:22), to dispute (9:29), to argue (17:2), to prove (17:3), to persuade (17:4), to confute powerfully (18:28).

The Belgic Confession sets forth this viewpoint in article 24: "We believe that this true faith, being wrought in man by the hearing of the Word of God and the operation of the Holy Ghost, doth regenerate and make him a new man, causing him to live a new life, and freeing him from the bondage of sin." Faith is wrought in man through the hearing of the gospel and its effectual application by the Holy Spirit. It is that simple. Throughout church history, beginning with Adam, the Holy Spirit applying the proclamation of the Word of God to the lost is what converts the elect. The Second London Baptist Confession states, "The gospel is the only outward means of revealing Christ and saving grace, and it is abundantly sufficient for that purpose" (20.4). This sentence encapsulates everything that needs to be said regarding biblical evangelism, which is simply to reveal Christ's saving grace to the lost. Such an approach is certain to be abundantly sufficient, regardless of salvific results, which is the point that needs to be emphasized.

This is not to say evangelism can be done only through auditory proclamation as opposed to some form of written medium. Any time the content of the gospel is communicated to an unbeliever, whether through a gospel tract, the Bible, or something else, evangelism is happening. But it does mean words are necessary, unlike what we see in many ministries today, where showing the gospel is equated with sharing it:

> Some people might say, "We don't have to say anything about the gospel. Our lifestyle will say it all." Others might quote the words of that old song, "They will know we are Christians by our love." Still others quote the words often wrongly attributed to Francis of Assisi (1181/82–1226), "Preach the gospel at all times—if necessary, use words." But we ought to look carefully again at Acts 11 to see what the church did there. Believers spoke of the wonderful grace of God in Christ…. They told people with words the good news about the Lord Jesus.[4]

Many Christians claim to believe what the Bible says about the power of the gospel to save, but when it comes to evangelism, you will rarely see them living this out. Many will pray for people to be saved without ever sharing the gospel with the people they

---

4. Wes Bredenhof, *To Win Our Neighbors for Christ* (Grand Rapids: Reformation Heritage Books, 2015), 48.

pray for. They will fly thousands of miles to build someone a house, trying to "share" the gospel by their deeds. They will spend months trying to establish a relationship with someone before sharing the demands of Christ.

These approaches are not wrong in themselves, but what is often left out is the communication of the gospel. Showing becomes equated with sharing, whereas in Scripture sharing the gospel has priority, even though our deeds and lifestyle should be consistent with the message. A disbelief in the power of the gospel to convert is something not seen in Scripture. John Owen agrees: "The way principally insisted on by the apostles was, by preaching the word itself unto them in the evidence and demonstration of the Spirit."[5] Even when derided or imprisoned by unbelievers, "yet they desisted not from pursuing their work in the same way; whereunto God gave success."[6]

After healing the lame beggar, Paul and Peter asked, "Men of Israel, why marvel ye at this? or why look ye so earnestly on us, as though by our own power or holiness we had made this man to walk?" (Acts 3:12). They pointed out that the healing was by Christ, not themselves. Likewise, God's working through the gospel saves people, not our behavior.

---

5. John Owen, *The Work of the Spirit* (1853; repr., Edinburgh.: Banner of Truth, 1967), 103.

6. Owen, *Work of the Spirit*, 103.

Our behavior can have a monumental impact on unbelievers, and we should strive to be holy as Christ is holy (1 Peter 1:16). But unless the Lord is drawing a person to the Son through the gospel, the unbeliever is likely to find fault in either our behavior or other Christians' behaviors if he is looking for an excuse not to believe. Even Jesus's life was nitpicked and found wanting by people who hated Him: "The Son of Man came eating and drinking, and they say, Behold a man gluttonous, and a winebibber, a friend of publicans and sinners" (Matt. 11:19). This demonstrates that if someone wants a reason not to believe, they will find it. It also demonstrates why a holy life, though important, is no replacement for gospel proclamation to the lost.

Many Christians also believe that sharing our testimony is a valid replacement for gospel proclamation. Testimonies in themselves are a wonderful supplement to the gospel and testify to Christ's saving work in our lives. They can be told in a way that points to Christ and the gospel. However, too often testimonies are used as a replacement for gospel proclamation. After all, who would deny that sharing a testimony is less offensive to the lost than the actual proclamation of the gospel? Testimonies can be used by Christians as a way to escape the offense of the cross. They can also be used to exalt the self, boasting in the sin we once loved or in the advancement we are now enjoying in Christ. This is not to condemn testimonies. It is merely to say that when it comes to evangelism, they should at best be supplemental to actual gospel proclamation.

Even biblical Christians can be influenced by unbiblical methods that neuter the offense of the cross. If we are not seeing people being saved or filling our churches, we have come to believe we are ineffective and should try something else. If someone is upset with us or calls us narrow-minded or bigoted when evangelizing, we are tempted to go about evangelism in a different, softer manner. This is not to say we should be obnoxious or profane when evangelizing. On the contrary, we should be respectful. Our genuine concern for the lost should be evident to all men. We should exude love for our hearers. But it is not to say our evangelism should become man-centered or pragmatic just because it does not see conversions. We should never resort to something other than the gospel.

On the face of it, evangelism is absurd. The cross is foolish. No one seeks God. The call to discipleship wrecks plans and goals, and this is why pragmatism is so tempting. But biblical evangelism is getting the gospel to people. Any other method can be attributed to a lack of faith in the gospel and a disbelief in the sufficiency of the Bible, which alone should be our guide for how to evangelize. Although holy lives and testimonies are helpful when it comes to evangelism, we must remember it pleases God to raise dead sinners through the foolishness of gospel proclamation (1 Cor. 1:18).

Reflection Questions

1. What is the gospel? Explain it as though you were speaking to a lost person.

2. How can a testimony point to the gospel of Christ?

3. Why are words necessary when sharing the gospel?

MYTH 3

Evangelism Is Unsuccessful If No One Is Converted

What is our aim when evangelizing? How do we define success? Is it conversions? Increased numbers coming to our churches? How many times we are arrested or mocked? Are we unsuccessful if any of these things don't take place?

We have just seen that God is sovereign in salvation, and the method He has given us for evangelism is gospel proclamation. But what is the goal of evangelism? This section addresses the natural outflow of the previous two myths. The Westminster Shorter Catechism states that the chief and highest end of man is to glorify God. This is also the chief and highest end of evangelism. Every time we share the gospel with the lost, God is glorified, whether or not a person is converted. The goal of evangelism is not to save the lost, since salvation is of the Lord. The goal of evangelism is to make Christ known.

Most Christians today are likely to define evangelism as something that yields results in the sphere of salvation or church growth. These things are unlikely to occur without evangelism taking place, but numerical yields of salvation and church growth should never be the aim of evangelism or ministry in general. Joel Osteen, Jehovah's Witnesses, and the Church of the Latter-Day Saints can grow a "church" numerically and get many converts. But this is no sign of doing it biblically.

Morton H. Smith observes, "Sometimes we think of evangelism as including the result…but evangelism should not be defined in terms of the results, rather, it should be defined in terms of the activity of setting forth the good news itself."[1] This is not to say conversions are unimportant, nor is it to say our motive for evangelizing is irrelevant. It is not to say evangelism should be without urgency or passion. But it is to say success in evangelism is defined by faithfulness to share the gospel, not how many converts are made.

J. I. Packer claims the confusion about "present-day debates" regarding evangelism can be attributed to "our widespread and persistent habit of defining evangelism in terms, not of a message delivered, but of an effect produced in our hearers."[2] Some have pointed out that a biblical view of evangelism is one of

---

1. Morton H. Smith, *Reformed Evangelism* (Clinton, Miss.: Multi-Communication Ministries, 1975), 4.

2. J. I. Packer, *Evangelism and the Sovereignty of God* (Downers Grove, Ill.: InterVarsity Press, 1961), 41.

the marks of a healthy church. This would imply that a church with a contrary view of evangelism would be unhealthy. So what is an example of an unbiblical view of evangelism? "One of the most common and dangerous mistakes is to confuse the results of evangelism with evangelism itself. This may be the most subtle of the misunderstandings. Evangelism must not be confused with the fruit of evangelism."[3]

For an example of evangelism seen through the lens of results, consider Darius Salter's comments in his book *American Evangelism*. He notes that Martin Luther defined evangelism as "nothing other than preaching, the speaking forth of God's grace and mercy, which the Lord Jesus Christ has earned and acquired through his death," and that Packer defines it as "just preaching the gospel, the evangel. It is the work of communication in which Christians make themselves the mouthpieces for God's message of mercy to sinners."[4] These definitions are wonderfully biblical, but Salter goes on to claim that "both Martin Luther's and J. I. Packer's definitions of evangelism are defective."[5] His reason is because "they leave no room for the evaluation of effectiveness."[6] By

---

3. Mark Dever, *Nine Marks of a Healthy Church* (Wheaton, Ill.: Crossway, 2000), 134.

4. Darius Salter, *American Evangelism* (Grand Rapids: Baker, 1996), 22–23.

5. Salter, *American Evangelism*, 23.

6. Salter, *American Evangelism*, 23.

effectiveness, Salter means success in conversions. It should not be a surprise, then, to find him later saying, "Evangelism has failed if it does not result in the evangelized ultimately being seated at the marriage supper of the Lamb."[7]

The view that the salvation of souls is not the chief end of evangelism has been criticized by many evangelicals. Critics such as "church growth" pundit Donald A. McGavron argue that "going everywhere and preaching the gospel" is not evangelism.[8] To be fair, evangelism should be concerned with discipleship and its connection to local churches, as will be seen in the last chapter of this book. But such concerns and connections do not qualify it as evangelism. McGavron disagrees, claiming such a view is simply a way to justify the lack of salvific success: "Christian missions needed a theology that would undergird it during the long years when it was weak at home and hard beset abroad."[9] He says in another place that because of small growth in church membership, such a view of evangelism is a way "to find a rationale for existence and continuance that did not depend on numbers of converts."[10]

---

7. Salter, *American Evangelism*, 29.

8. Donald A. McGavran, *Understanding Church Growth* (Grand Rapids: Eerdmans, 1970), 24.

9. McGavran, *Understanding Church Growth*, 24.

10. McGavran, *Understanding Church Growth*, 26.

McGavran is not alone in his assumption, although the division is usually made along theological lines. Synergists take the approach that conversion is partly a product of man's cooperation or choice, and thus salvific results are necessary if it is to be called evangelism. They believe we should be able to achieve such salvific results through mere persuasion, persistence, and human ingenuity. Reformed Christians, as we have seen, believe salvation is a product of God alone even though He uses means to accomplish this purpose. Salvation is not something that can be scientifically manipulated since God alone grants faith.

When it comes to conversion, the most difficult area of all Christianity to evaluate, we must leave such assumptions to God, who alone "looketh on the heart" (1 Sam. 16:7) and who alone grants faith to the unbeliever. In the parable of the soils or sower, Christ warns us of assuming persons are saved merely because of excitement, emotion, or even apparent ebullience about the gospel (Matt. 13:18–23). Only the Lord converts, and only the Lord knows the true state of a person's relationship with God, so how could we use conversion as a reliable guide about whether our evangelism is successful?

The Bible also shows that evangelism will often result in a gospel call that is not efficacious, yet it is still successful since this was God's will for it. This is presupposed when Christ says, "He that believeth and is baptized shall be saved; but he that believeth not shall be damned" (Mark 16:16). Ernest C. Reisinger points out that even damnation is a result of evangelism, and hence it is effective even when none are saved: "There are two results: 'he that believeth and is baptized shall be saved'…. And 'he that believeth not shall be damned.' Salvation is one result, and damnation is another result."[11] One paragraph later he states, "When the biblical gospel is preached, there will be results, and God will be glorified…His justice, holiness, and righteousness will be glorified in the damnation of those who believe not. Many modern preachers do not like even to mention this aspect of the results, but it is clear in the Bible. When God reveals His mercy, He always reveals His judgment, and the Bible makes this very clear."

This means evangelism is always effective regardless of how a person responds, since the Lord is glorified either way.

Packer notes, "The way to tell whether in fact you are evangelizing is not to ask whether conversions are known to have resulted from your witness. It is to ask whether you are faithfully making known the gospel message."[12] George W. Robertson agrees in his booklet *What Is Evangelism?* "The Bible never hints that the herald is the converter. Persuasion or conversion

---

11. Ernest C. Reisinger, *Today's Evangelism* (Phillipsburg, N.J.: Craig Press, 1982), 11.

12. Packer, *Evangelism and the Sovereignty of God*, 41.

is possible only when the Spirit removes 'a heart of stone' and replaces it with a 'heart of flesh' (Ezek. 36:26) and 'opens' it to receive the free offer of grace (Acts 16:40)."[13] Conversion is something no human could ever do to another human. What we are called to do is share the gospel, which the Lord shows to be the proper method for evangelism.

We must declare the gospel to all the world, including the call that "all men every where" should repent (Acts 17:30). We must wrestle with men's souls, pleading that they be reconciled to God through Jesus Christ (2 Cor. 5:20). We must tell men to "choose you this day whom ye will serve" (Josh. 24:15), though the effectual call of the gospel is a work of God alone. God is sovereign in all things, especially salvation, even though He condescends to use "the foolishness of preaching to save them that believe" (1 Cor. 1:21). We must preach the cross and resurrection. We must preach faith in Jesus Christ, bidding sinners to come to Him, knowing that all the while salvation is a gift of God: "No man can come to me, except the Father which hath sent me draw him…. No man can come unto me, except it were given unto him of my Father" (John 6:44, 65).

William Carey provides a remarkable example of faithfulness despite few conversions during the

---

13. George W. Robertson, *What Is Evangelism?* (Phillipsburg, N.J.: P&R Publishing, 2013), 6.

early days of ministry in India: "I am very fruitless and almost useless but the Word and the attributes of God are my hope, and my confidence, and my joy, and I trust that his glorious designs will undoubtedly be answered."[14] Iain Murray remarks of Carey, "The obstacles were immense. Problems of poverty and illness, overshadowed by the darker burden of a land where in Carey's words, 'ten thousand ministers would find scope for their powers,' were constantly with them. Through the first five and a half years they saw not a single Indian convert."[15] Jesus himself saw few converts after three years of ministry. The same could be said of the prophets of old, especially Isaiah and Jeremiah. They were specifically told by the Lord that their preaching would see few or no converts. These men continued to press on anyway. They didn't believe they were unsuccessful, even if they weren't satisfied with the little fruit they did see. They kept going, knowing it is God who gives the increase.

The Christian who faithfully shares the gospel from a motive of love for God and love for man can never be a failure when evangelizing. He may never see anyone saved. He may never receive an invitation to speak at a conference. He may never see a crowd

---

14. William Carey to Mary Carey and Ann Hobson, December 22, 1796, in *The Journal and Selected Letters of William Carey*, ed. Terry G. Carter (Macon, Ga.: Smyth & Helwys, 2000), 249.

15. Iain H. Murray, *The Puritan Hope* (Edinburgh: Banner of Truth, 1971), 140.

when preaching in the open air. He may never have any statistics to boast of in his newsletter or denomination report. His church may not grow. But if he is faithful to the biblical prescription for evangelism, he is successful. This is not to say we should be satisfied with empty nets. It is to say, however, that the mark of "successful" evangelism should never be the number of conversions or how many people rush to the messenger or his church. This is why Paul was successful despite failing in the eyes of the world.

Reflection Questions

1. Why do many Christians believe that the goal of evangelism is conversions? Are they correct?

2. Why is our motive so important when evangelizing, even if success is simply sharing the gospel with the lost?

3. Is it possible that someone you have shared Christ with was later converted without you knowing it? Do you think this is a common phenomenon?

MYTH 4

The Lost Should Never Be Offended by Our Evangelism

We live in a culture in which offending someone is the worst of crimes. Toleration is the new religion. Peaceful coexistence is the new mantra. But what does this mean for our approach to the lost? Is it possible to evangelize without offending anyone? And if we do offend someone, have we spoiled our witness? What happens if the lost get mad at us for evangelizing? Is there a way to avoid this and still be biblical?

This again is why theology is so important. The Scriptures teach that unbelieving man is hostile in his mind against God (Rom. 8:7). Unbelievers see the message of the cross as foolishness (1 Cor. 1:18). The god of this world has blinded unbelievers' minds so that they see no glory in the gospel but are rather enraged against it, whether or not this rage manifests itself openly (2 Cor. 4:4). The one sharing the gospel will be an aroma of death to the unbeliever (2 Cor. 2:16).

When the early church was taking root, there were no critiques when it came to evangelism's divisiveness. The evangelism of the early church was explosive. It was bold and direct. Yet no one in the church is ever seen condemning it. There was never a meeting among elders to discuss whether they should go about evangelizing in such a brash manner, especially considering the offense it caused. People lost not only jobs but houses as well (Heb. 10:34). People were harried from city to city as well as stoned and crucified.

To illustrate this, consider Paul's approach to evangelism while in Cyprus (Acts 13:4–12). As Paul and Barnabas go through the whole island (v. 6), they encounter "a false prophet, a Jew, whose name was Barjesus" or "Elymas" (vv. 6, 8). After the false prophet opposes them, "seeking to turn away the deputy from the faith" (v. 8), Paul goes on to proclaim the following words: "Thou child of the devil, thou enemy of all righteousness, wilt thou not cease to pervert the right ways of the Lord?" (v. 10). Not stopping there, Paul even blinds the man through "the hand of the Lord" (v. 11). This last phrase is interesting because it indicates the Lord was clearly in approval of such measures, just as in the beginning, before Paul begins his diatribe, we are told he is "filled with the Holy Ghost" (v. 9).

Although some in today's church would call this offensive and mean-spirited, Barnabas never condemns Paul. When Paul is later beaten, stoned, and chased out of cities, something that might offend most Christians today, the church never turns its back on Paul for being too scandalous or unloving. Christians often have the mindset that if we are going to be relevant in the culture, we must keep quiet outside our homes and churches about the gospel or, at the very least, come up with ways and methods that will allow evangelism to be inoffensive. We don't want to be judgmental or intolerant. We don't want our churches to have a bad reputation. Christians today are often fearful of what outsiders think of us. This can create the assumption that evangelism is best done in ways that do not arouse hostility, and whenever it does, the person responsible should be disciplined or at least rebuked on account of it. The Christian community often considers any kind of scandal or outrage from the unbelieving world to be a mark of woeful ineffectiveness.

This was never the case with Paul and the early church. The Scriptures show that this kind of response to the gospel is expected from those dead in sin as well as from professing Christians who have not submitted to God's Word in this area. The early church "emblazoned on its banners its loathing and disdain for the cults."[1] It never sought "the friendship

---

1. Herbert B. Workman, *Persecution in the Early Church* (Bloomington, Ill.: Clearnote Press, 2014), 65.

of the world" (James 4:4). It did not love the world or the things in the world (1 John 2:15). Naturally this led Christians to the lions or to the stake, but in doing so, paradoxically, it also conquered the world as people began to notice such boldness. The world realized this was something different from other religions, which were typically tolerant and inclusive.

The cross will always appear foolish to those who are perishing because it attacks people in their pride—whether intellectual, physical, monetary, or spiritual. This is also why we have a natural tendency to shrink from conflict and to condemn anyone who brings conflict on the church when evangelizing. But we must never forget it is through the foolishness of preaching, not catering to man's will, that dead men come alive. Softening the cross with clever speech or eloquence can only create false converts who are drawn to the cleverness or eloquence rather than Christ (1 Cor. 2:1–2). Trying to bring the gospel to unbelievers in compromised ways can only lead to the hardening of the unbeliever, which in turn justifies his rebellion against God.

It does not mean the Christian should intentionally antagonize or look for such a response while evangelizing. It does not mean the Christian should dismiss advice or correction when it comes to evangelism, especially when coming from his local church. The Christian should never intentionally try to look foolish or provoke people's ire. He should not try to prove himself by seeing how many people want to kill him. But anyone faithfully sharing the Word of God will encounter a stiff-necked and adulterous generation and the typical responses generated because of it.

It is often assumed if the culture or individuals are upset by our evangelism, such reproach won't gain converts and we should try another method. But reproach and scoffing are exactly the responses we should expect when it comes to biblical evangelism, as are arrests and confiscation of property. In fact, why would we assume any other response? The world's eyes are veiled to the gospel (2 Cor. 4:3). There are none who seek God (Rom. 3:11).

The idea that any kind of hostility against Christians is a bad thing for the church, even if induced by evangelism, has betrayed the church's misunderstanding of what happens when the gospel is faithfully proclaimed to the lost. In a hardened atmosphere like the contemporary West, hatred from the world will typically happen far more often than the conversion of "the one." While the church welcomes the conversion of the one, it generally does not welcome the hatred of the world. This is something that needs to be reevaluated in light of scriptural truth.

Even Jesus was threatened with death on numerous occasions for His evangelism. The first time He preached, He was led to "the brow of the hill whereon their city was built, that they might cast him down headlong" (Luke 4:29). Another time "the Jews took up stones again to stone him" (John 10:31). His disciples followed in a similar path after Jesus had ascended. This is not to say evangelism should intentionally offend the unbeliever, but the Scriptures are clear that the exclusivity of Christ and the demand of the gospel are offensive in themselves, and the one sharing will be made "a spectacle unto the world" (1 Cor. 4:9). When evangelizing, the Christian must remember the words of the Master: "If the world hate you, ye know that it hated me before it hated you" (John 15:18). Instead of shrinking back, we should rejoice, knowing our trials are going toward the advancement of God's kingdom.

When it comes to evangelism, things are not getting easier in the West. The culture's hatred of biblical Christianity is becoming more pronounced. Yet the church is oftentimes ashamed or offended by the righteous scandal that evangelism provokes. If the church is upset now whenever evangelism causes an offense, what will happen when things get even worse? In attempting to accommodate our evangelism to the culture, we have lost the appeal of being a savor of death to the dying (2 Cor. 2:16). As noisome as such an odor is, it is still going to bring an awareness of the gospel, whether or not it is believed. The early Christians were successful in part because of their utter disregard of what the culture thought about them, even in the face of persecution.

These are the days when the churches in the West must train Christians to preach Christ in the teeth of persecution and death. We must seek to turn the world upside down with the gospel. We must stir things up not obnoxiously, but boldly and without shame of the scandal that the gospel causes. We conclude this chapter with Louis Berkhof's rousing call to arms:

> The Church…is duty bound to carry on an incessant warfare against the hostile world in every form in which it reveals itself, whether in the Church or outside of it, and against all spiritual forces of darkness. The Church may not spend all her time in prayer and meditation, however necessary and important these may be, nor may she rest on her oars in the peaceful enjoyment of her spiritual heritage. She must be engaged with all her might in the battles of her Lord, fighting in a war that is both offensive and defensive.[2]

---

2. Louis Berkhof, *Systematic Theology* (Edinburgh: Banner of Truth, 1958), 565.

Reflection Questions

1. What's the difference between the gospel offending an unbeliever and our behavior or tone offending an unbeliever?

2. What does Paul mean when he says we are an aroma of death to the unbeliever (2 Cor. 2:15–17)?

3. Are unbelievers really offended whenever they hear the gospel, even if they don't show it or seem like it?

MYTH 5

There's Only One Right Way to Evangelize

The gospel and intercessory prayer should be the focus of our evangelism, but does this mean we can't do it in a variety of ways or contexts? Is one method better than another if both are gospel-centered? How do we know which way is the best or right way?

Evangelism can be done in a variety of ways and in a variety of contexts while still being biblical. For example, open air preaching can be done in cities and countries where such a form of proselytizing is allowed and where people are walking around. In other places, such as India and China, it would not currently be advised. In countries more tolerant of Christianity, one-on-one evangelism can be done at work, when talking to friends or relatives, or even to a stranger at a supermarket. The Lord opens doors in different ways when it comes to evangelism. He uses our different personalities and backgrounds. No method should be treated as the best, nor should any method be frowned on, assuming the gospel has priority in the encounter.

How should we establish what approach to evangelism is best in a given context or given certain spiritual giftings? Paul asks people to pray that the Lord would open doors for him to share the gospel (Col. 4:3). Oftentimes the Lord did. In other places, however, the Lord did not open doors for Paul but rather closed them (Acts 16:6). The Lord is faithful to give Christians opportunities to share about Christ, but it is up to us, led by the Holy Spirit, to recognize when and how to do it. Open air preaching can be effective where there is a large gathering of people on public or city property. However, this should be restricted only to qualified men, as we see in Scripture. At other times, the Lord will open doors while we talk to strangers or while at work. These opportunities typically come out of nowhere, which is why we must be ready in season and out of season. At other times, such as on a plane or bus, we may intentionally engage in conversation with someone we don't know for the sake of trying to turn the conversation to Christ.

Our different spheres in life and the relationships the Lord has sovereignly orchestrated for us provide ample opportunity to share about the Lord. Sometimes we will be brought into contact with people every day, such as those in our families. At other times we may see the person only once in our lives.

Such scenarios will demand different approaches. Christians have a purpose for every relationship we have. We are called to love our neighbor as ourselves, and the best way to love them is to talk to them about their soul. George Whitefield is famous for his open air preaching exploits, but he is also a man who didn't go fifteen minutes in a conversation without speaking to his interlocutor about Christ. This should be our aim, considering how important it is to be reconciled to God and how weighty such a topic as the gospel is.

We should strive to be gracious toward other Christians in their different approaches to the lost. People are gifted by the Lord in different ways and have different burdens or different desires when it comes to their dealings with the lost. Some people prefer having supper with lost neighbors, praying for an open door through such an event. Some prefer preaching on the streets. Some like arranging events through their churches, hoping to bring the gospel to the lost in that way. Some prefer handing out tracts or leaving them in restaurants or bookstores. Evangelism is not something to be done in a straight-jacketed manner. Assuming we are staying within the perimeter of Scripture and our method is gospel proclamation and prayer, it would be unfair to call our way better than someone else's. Paul rejoiced the gospel was being preached, whether in pretense or in truth (Phil. 1:18). This is not to say we should be willing to accept false gospels or unbiblical methods, but we should be patient and reasonable when hearing about how others evangelize.

The following are some approaches to evangelism currently in vogue. This is not a blanket endorsement of these kinds of evangelism but rather a guide to be used if the Christian ever encounters such terminology. There are advantages and disadvantages to each approach, as will be demonstrated.[1]

First, *relational* or *lifestyle evangelism* attempts to intentionally develop relationships with the lost for the purpose of sharing the gospel at a later and more appropriate time. Much of this approach emphasizes showing the gospel rather than sharing it. Such an approach can make it easier to keep up with the person since it is not as confrontational or offensive as other, more direct approaches. This can help evangelism seem more natural and organic. The downsides of such a method are numerous, however. It saps the urgency to share the gospel. It waits for the right time, even though if we listen to our flesh, there is never a right time. It will always be difficult to open our mouths about Christ, which this approach seems to justify. It can eliminate certain groups from getting the gospel, since relationships are subjective. For instance, no one wants to start a friendship with a

---

1. Thanks to Dr. Timothy Beougher of The Southern Baptist Theological Seminary for sharing some of these methods.

leper or a homeless person, even though we should seek to get the gospel to these people as well. It is also deceptive and manipulative since the relationship isn't really about the person but rather a hidden motive only to be revealed later. It is also anthropocentric since the focus is on the Christian's behavior rather than Christ's.

Second, *servant evangelism* is an attempt to share Christ by modeling biblical servanthood. The idea is to share the love of God through practical action such as giving out water bottles, offering up prayer, or building homes. This approach can help believers become more comfortable with evangelism. It intentionally goes outside the church to encounter the lost. It is an attempt to follow Christ's example of serving others rather than being served. It attempts to show the world that the church isn't some corrupted or money-hungry enterprise but is actually concerned about helping the lost materially as well as spiritually. The problem with this approach is that without the gospel, it is not evangelism. Such an approach often deviates into social ministry that, in essence, is no different from what humane or even atheistic societies do. Giving out water bottles, praying for people, and even building homes are nice things to do, but they cannot be substituted for evangelism, which is the proclamation of Christ and a call to believe, as we have seen.

Third, *confrontational* or *cold-call evangelism* shares the gospel with strangers without any previous encounter with them. Examples would include door-to-door evangelism or open air preaching. It could also include walking up to people and directly asking them about their relationship with the Lord. The advantage of this approach is it makes certain that people hear the gospel. It is urgent. It is intentionally gospel-centered. It is exemplified in the Bible, especially in Acts. It is a good way to teach Christians to evangelize. It helps crucify the fear of man. It is a kind of on-the-job training. Some disadvantages of such an approach is that it can seem insensitive. Follow-ups or maintaining contact with those evangelized is difficult. It can also make it easier for the Christian to not live consistently with the gospel he preaches, since the strangers don't know him.

These are just some of the more popular approaches to evangelism today. Each can be used in a way that is biblical, and each can deviate in ways that would not be biblical. At the end of the day, the best method is the one consistent with Scripture and in accordance with whatever context a person finds himself in. It is important to remember evangelism is communicating the gospel with language, even though our love for Christ should compel us to also provide an example of biblical living. Our role as Christians must keep us from devolving into ministries that look more like human societies or governmental handouts rather than intentional gospel witness. What the lost need is to be reconciled to God, first and foremost, and this is what biblical evangelism seeks to convey—otherwise it's not really loving our neighbors.

Reflection Questions

1. How can we discern if the Lord has opened a door for evangelizing?

2. How can we know which approach to evangelism is the best, given that there are multiple approaches that are gospel-focused?

3. Are there any approaches of biblical evangelism not mentioned here? Is there one that you favor above others? If so, why?

MYTH 6

Evangelism and Apologetics Are Different

What is apologetics? Is it only for trained academics or spiritual elites? Is it to be used only as "pre-evangelism"? What is the best way to do apologetics, and does our approach really matter? Is apologetics even necessary when evangelizing?

The notion that apologetics is to be used as "pre-evangelism" is misleading and unbiblical. It assumes that before we can actually share the gospel, the person must get to the place where he believes in God, the historical person of Jesus, and a biblical understanding of sin and evil. It assumes the gospel is something distinct from belief in God, the Scriptures, and the historical person of Jesus. It suggests a person must get to a place intellectually where he becomes more open to receiving the good news of the cross and resurrection. As we have seen, however, a person's mind is corrupted by the fall. He is not simply lacking information. It is his entire way of thinking that must be regenerated if he is to believe the gospel.

Apologetics and evangelism go hand in hand. Apologetics, or defending the faith (1 Peter 3:15), will always be necessary when evangelizing. This is because evangelism is an intentional effort to expose the inconsistency of another person's worldview or belief system while at the same time demonstrating the consistency of what the Scriptures teach and proclaim. This is exactly what biblical apologetics also seeks to do.

The most biblical approach to apologetics is what is called *presuppositional apologetics*.[1] This is a distinctively Reformed apologetic that begins and ends with the God of the Scriptures. It does not seek to put the Scriptures away until a more "opportune" time. This is in accordance with the demand to set Christ apart as Lord over everything we do, including apologetics. "It assumes Christianity's truth at the outset and then challenges the natural man by demonstrating that on his presuppositions nothing is true, nothing can be accounted for, and his own thinking is invalid."[2] Presuppositional apologetics aims to demonstrate that

---

1. Cornelius Van Til, Greg Bahnsen, Gordon Clark, and Francis Schaeffer are generally considered leading presuppositional apologists, although the tradition began much earlier with John Calvin, Augustine, and, most importantly, with the authors of Scripture.

2. Rousas John Rushdoony, *By What Standard* (Vallecito, Calif.: Ross House, 1995), 100.

Christianity is the only valid worldview that exists, and it is impossible for it not to be true.

The Christian must labor to show that the unbeliever's worldview will always be untenable or inconsistent with what he or she claims to believe. The Christian must then turn the tables by pointing out, in contrast, that Christianity is the only worldview consistent with what it claims. The unbeliever must be shown that his worldview cannot make sense of reality without borrowing from Christian presuppositions. For instance, logic, science, mathematics, morality, and other disciplines cannot be valid or justified or even functional unless grounded on the objective, eternal, unchangeable God of the Bible. Likewise, any interpretation of reality must be thoroughly Christian if it is to be accurate or consistent, since Christ has made all things and is the only way man's redemption is possible.

All people have a personal worldview or commitment that acts as chief authority in their life. This is what the Christian must drive home and expose when evangelizing. An unbeliever's authority will be himself or some other mistake-prone human, and it will always prove inconsistent with what it claims. Ever since Adam ate the forbidden fruit, men have tried to make themselves God. Naturally hostile in mind toward God (1 Cor. 1:21), they consider themselves to be the ultimate criterion of truth and set themselves up as knowing the universe better than

God. They reference everything in light of their own reason or desire, which of course is debilitated by sin. Adam and Eve did the same thing when they bit into the fruit, but without God as a reference, how can the unbeliever be certain his reason is even valid? Where does such a thing come from without God? How can he even assume to know anything at all? How can reason, knowledge, truth, and consciousness come from inert, lifeless, truthless material? This is the folly of making one's self the standard of truth. It always proves to be inconsistent with reality.

Biblical apologetics demonstrates to the unbeliever the irrationality and even impossibility of all other worldviews other than historic Christianity: "The way to prove the truth of Christianity, then, is to take the conflicting worldviews of the Christian and the non-Christian—with their opposing presuppositions and theories of knowledge, in terms of which particular claims are disputed back and forth—and press for a critical internal analysis of each one, looking for philosophical inconsistency and absurdity. This is the way to refute the unbeliever's bedrock presuppositions, showing the intellectual impossibility of any worldview that is contrary to Christianity."[3]

The Scriptures must be the ultimate criterion of truth for every Christian, and no less so when doing

3. Greg Bahnsen, *Van Til's Apologetic* (Phillipsburg, N.J.: P&R Publishing, 1998), 701.

apologetics. Many Christians claim that the Bible is the ultimate criterion for truth but then compromise when defending or contending for the faith. They will take a more "neutral" position when it comes to Scripture. But a Christian must stand on the authority of the Bible in every aspect of his life, which includes dealing with unbelievers.

Ever since God spoke to Adam in Paradise before the fall, He has used supernatural communication to deal with His people.[4] This is the case even though sinners, apart from the Holy Spirit, will always attempt to eradicate or twist God's Word. Biblical apologetics does not ask the unbeliever to consider the possibility of the Bible's authority. It begins with the Bible as self-authoritative and self-attesting, and it claims that without such revelation, no meaningful interpretation of anything could be possible. Because of our finite knowledge and proclivity to sin, we must use the Bible to interpret the universe. Christ as God speaks in the Bible with absolute authority. Thus, the Bible does not appeal to human reason for its justification, otherwise humans would be positioned as more authoritative than God's Word. Rather, the Bible comes to the human being with absolute authority and demands that men submit to it.

---

4. "The Bible is the supernatural communication of God to creatures who have become sinners." Bahnsen, *Van Til's Apologetic*, 713.

The Christian must never give up the Bible as the ultimate reference point in evangelism, because nothing is more authoritative than God's Word. God appeals to Himself as the ultimate authority (Heb. 6:16), since to appeal to anything else would make that thing more authoritative than God. Anything inconsistent with the Bible is wrong because the Bible, as God's revelation, is always the ultimate authority, not man. The Bible as God's revelation is sufficient, infallible, and inerrant since it comes from an eternal, perfect Being who created and sustains the universe. Because of our finite knowledge and proclivity to sin, we must use the Bible to interpret the universe, otherwise our interpretation will be wrong.

The Christian must internally examine whatever worldview is being presented from the viewpoint of that religion. By doing so, it will become evident that contradictions exist between what a person claims to believe and how that claim actually matches up to reality. Religions that stem from or have been influenced by the Bible, such as Islam, Mormonism, or Jehovah's Witnesses, can be treated as Christian heresies and reasoned against by using Scripture itself to show where they have departed from the truth.

Although it is helpful to have an understanding of other religions and cults when defending or contending for the faith, it is just as useful to have a grasp of biblical doctrine and church history. Being able to clearly articulate orthodox doctrine or certain contexts of church history will be useful against most world religions or cults, which are usually by-products if not duplications of prior heretical movements.[5] Knowledge of church history will help a believer identify such heresies and know how the Christians of old defended the faith against them. This is why the Christian would best spend his time studying doctrine and church history rather than evidential arguments for the existence of God or other Christian truth claims. He would also benefit from studying the specific religions or cults he is likely to engage, which include Darwinian evolution, Marxism, militant veganism, and other groups that would deny being explicitly religious.

The Christian must also be sensitive to sincere questions when evangelizing the lost, as opposed to those intended to stump him. Like Satan, the unbeliever will often twist the Scriptures in an attempt to make the Christian contradict himself. Spending time with such persons could be an example of casting "pearls before swine" (Matt. 7:6), although this is not always the case. When encountering someone who is sincerely wrestling or having difficulty with some doctrine of the faith, such as the resurrection or the virgin birth, using Scripture instead of classical

---

5. This includes Islam and even Marxism, both of which are spin-offs in many ways of orthodox Christianity.

or evidential approaches is advised since there is no higher authority than Scripture.

Every Christian should make a serious, self-conscious effort to become better prepared to "be ready always to give an answer to every man that asketh you a reason of the hope that is in you" and to do so in a way that presents Christ as set apart or sanctified as Lord God in your hearts (1 Peter 3:15). Every Christian must contend for the faith (Phil. 1:7; Jude 3) as he is given opportunity. Apologetics is not only for the specialized theologian or minister. It is not something only academic or elite Christians do. It is something every Christian does any time biblical evangelism takes place, whether or not the Christian is aware of it.

Reflection Questions

1. How can knowledge of church history be useful when engaging in apologetics?

2. How would our approach to an atheist or agnostic be different from our approach to a follower of a cult or world religion?

3. What is meant by the "presuppositional method" of apologetics? How would you explain it to another Christian?

MYTH 7

Reformed Christians Don't Evangelize

Thus far we have seen why anything other than Reformed theology will lead to pragmatism, false conversions, watered-down gospel presentations, and inappropriate approaches to apologetics. But what about the claim that Reformed Christians don't evangelize? What about hyper-Calvinism? If God is sovereign in salvation and already has elected people whom He will invariably save, what's the point of evangelism or missions?

The Lord uses means to accomplish His ends and purposes, and it is no less so when it comes to evangelism. Even though God is sovereign, He has decreed to use human instruments to accomplish His work of saving the lost, since it is humans who bring the gospel to others. This is why evangelism is such a privilege. We have been entrusted with the gospel of Jesus Christ and have been assigned as God's ambassadors. Is this not enough to motivate us to be active in evangelism?

Some think belief in the doctrine of God's unconditional election will produce a lack of zeal in evangelism, but history shows the opposite: "This doctrine does not hinder the work of mission, but powerfully energizes it. Through the preaching of men the elect will be gathered in. Therefore, the gospel must be preached by men!"[1] Wes Bredenhof observes that "even when the mission work of the church does not appear successful from a human perspective, God's purposes will never be frustrated. Whether through one missionary or another, whether through one sermon or another, through whatever means He chooses, God will gather His elect."[2]

This is why Stephen Lawson can show that the history of evangelism is filled with men who believed in the doctrines of grace:

> Far from paralyzing these spiritual giants, the doctrines of grace kindled within their hearts a reverential awe for God that humbled their souls before His throne. The truths of divine sovereignty emboldened these men to rise up and advance the cause of Christ on earth…. The doctrines of grace ignited them to serve God in their divinely appointed hour of history, leaving a godly inheritance for future generations.[3]

---

1. Bredenhof, *To Win Our Neighbors for Christ*, 82.
2. Bredenhof, *To Win Our Neighbors for Christ*, 83.
3. Stephen J. Lawson, introduction to *The Missionary Fellowship*

Speaking about William Carey, Lawson says, "He also put the lie to the notion that Calvinism and missions don't mix. Far from holding to a view of God's sovereignty that sees no place for missions and evangelism, Carey was consumed with passion for God's power to convert sinners as revealed in the gospel."[4] Andrew Fuller, the Reformed preacher whom Spurgeon considered the "greatest theologian" of the nineteenth century, not only gave hearty approval of world evangelism but contended it could be done only through "God's time-honored method of planting churches and winning the lost."[5] Contrary to popular caricatures, John Calvin himself was zealous about evangelism and did more for the promotion of the gospel than most of his critics:

> Calvin made Geneva the base camp for an intensive evangelistic effort in France. Between 1555 and 1562 Calvin and his colleagues sent eighty-eight evangelists to France. God blessed their efforts because by 1559 the Huguenots French Calvinists numbered over one hundred thousand. In 1555 Calvin commissioned a missionary

---

of *William Carey* (Sanford, Fla.: Reformation Trust Publishing, 2018), xii.

4. Lawson, introduction, xiii.

5. Michael A. G. Haykin, *The Missionary Fellowship of William Carey* (Sanford, Fla.: Reformation Trust Publishing, 2018), 57.

to go to Brazil. All of this reflected Calvin's understanding of the Great Commission."[6]

During these days, Calvin wrote a personal letter to Heinrich Bullinger on October 1, 1560: "In Normandy our brethren are preaching in public, because no private house is capable of containing an audience of three or four thousand persons."[7] When commenting on Matthew 28:19, Calvin said, "The boundaries of Judea were prescribed to the prophets under the law, but now the wall is pulled down and the Lord orders the ministers of the gospel to go far out to scatter the teaching of salvation throughout all the regions of the earth."[8]

This is the mindset the Puritans inherited as well. Far from being cold and stodgy, they were energetic and excited about saving souls. Open air preaching on the streets of London was a common occurrence in the 1500s, as described by the Puritan John Jewel: "Sometimes at Paul's Cross six-thousand persons were sitting together, which was very grievous to the

---

6. John Mark Terry, *Evangelism: A Concise History* (New York: Broadman & Holman, 1994), 79.

7. John Calvin, *John Calvin Tracts and Letters*, ed. Henry Beveridge (Edinburgh: Banner of Truth, 2009), 7:137.

8. Timothy George, "The Challenges of Evangelism in the History of the Church," in *Evangelism in the Twenty-First Century*, ed. Thom Rainer (Wheaton, Ill.: Harold Shaw Publishers, 1989), 14.

papists."[9] These were not the days of religious freedom, yet the forerunners of the Puritan movement were out in the highways and byways, compelling people to come in. They risked their lives for the sake of telling others the true gospel. Such a burden for souls among the Puritans can also be seen in what is now called evangelistic literature, which the Puritans invented.[10] Joseph Alleine's *Alarm to the Unconverted* and Richard Baxter's *Call to the Unconverted* are two examples from the thousands of tracts or books written with the aim of converting the lost. The same could be said of the many treatises Puritans wrote dealing with the conscience.

Another writer notes that "the greatest evangelists in the history of the Christian church have believed that salvation is by God's election." The writer then goes on to name George Whitefield, Jonathan Edwards, William Carey, Adoniram Judson, Charles Spurgeon, D. Martyn Lloyd-Jones, and Francis Schaeffer as examples.[11] Speaking about the life of historic Reformed Christians, Hughes Oliphant Old writes, "The spirituality of God's eternal purposes has often led to an evangelistic, missionary spirituality."[12]

9. Murray, *Puritan Hope*, 6.

10. J. I. Packer, *Quest for Godliness* (Wheaton, Ill.: Crossway, 1990), 291.

11. Dever, *Nine Marks of a Healthy Church*, 151.

12. Hughes Oliphant Old, "What Is Reformed Spirituality? Played Over Again Lightly," in *Calvin Studies VII*, ed. John H.

One unsung hero of Reformed evangelism is John Eliot (1604–1690), who "strove to plant Christ's monarchy among his Christianized Indians as a model for God's rule among the nations."[13] Eliot's evangelism among the Indians in the New World saw thousands of conversions, along with nineteen towns of Indian natives who had believed the gospel and made a covenant "to give themselves and their children to God to be his people as the basis of a new civil government."[14] Not stopping there, Eliot translated the Bible into the language of the Native Americans among whom he was laboring. When accosted by a knife-wielding Native American chief, Eliot said, "I am about the great work of God, and He is with me, so that I fear not all the sachems [chiefs] of the country. I'll go on and you touch me if you dare."[15] David Brainerd is another missionary to the Native Americans who was an adamant believer and preacher of God's electing grace. Brainerd devoted his short life to spreading the gospel despite daunting odds.

When discussing the Protestant Reformation, historian Carlos Eire credits the international influence of Calvinists to the fact that they "did not just

---

Leith, Colloquium on Calvin Studies (Davidson, N.C.: Davidson College, 1994), 68.

13. Joel Beeke and Mark Jones, *A Puritan Theology* (Grand Rapids: Reformation Heritage Books, 2017), 784.

14. Beeke and Jones, *Puritan Theology*, 785.

15. Beeke and Jones, *Puritan Theology*, 785.

theorize; they were also eager to overthrow false religion and any ruler who defended it."[16] Is this not a missionary spirit? Is this not an active evangelistic enterprise? Eire acknowledges that "Calvinists tended to be…bent on continual growth. And wherever they surfaced, their activism would kick into high gear."[17] Eire records that Calvinism spread to Scotland, England, Germany, Hungary, Poland, and Lithuania within the span of roughly fifty years.[18]

Consider also that at the essence of Romans 9, one of the most illuminating texts in all of Scripture when it comes to unconditional election or predestination, Paul's heart breaks for the reprobate: "I have great heaviness and continual sorrow in my heart. For I could wish that myself were accursed from Christ for my brethren, my kinsmen according to the flesh" (vv. 2–3). In the next chapter, rather than excusing their damnation or dismissing them as already predestined to judgment, he says, "My heart's desire and prayer to God for Israel is, that they might be saved" (10:1). He goes on to give us the means of their salvation, if it is to take place: "And how shall they hear without a preacher?… So then faith cometh by hearing, and hearing by the word of God" (vv. 14, 17). Paul's high view of God's sovereignty does not keep

---

16. Carlos M. N. Eire, *Reformations* (New Haven, Conn.: Yale University Press, 2016), 312.

17. Eire, *Reformations*, 312.

18. Eire, *Reformations*, 312–14.

him bound within the confines of the church or the study. He doesn't cast off his responsibility to evangelize but is rather motivated all the more to go out, that the lost might hear and be saved.

Reformed theology keeps the Christian from being discouraged and proud. It keeps the focus on the glory of God. It is trusting that the Lord's sheep will hear the voice of their Master as we evangelize. It is knowing that, even if none are saved by our efforts, God is still glorified. The notion that Reformed Christians don't evangelize is one of the most common mischaracterizations in modern evangelicalism today. True enough, some Reformed Christians are not passionate about evangelism, but the same goes for many Arminian believers as well. It is not a particular soteriology that keeps people from witnessing but rather our own sin and selfishness. But as church history shows, Reformed theology produces men and women who are zealous to bring the good news of Christ to the lost, knowing that when they do so, even if it costs them their lives, they can never fail—God's sheep will hear His voice.

Reflection Questions

1. What Reformed evangelists, preachers, or Christians can you think of who are not mentioned in this section?

2. Do you find in your own experience that Calvinists are more eager to evangelize than non-Calvinists? Why (or why not) is that the case?

3. How does evangelizing for the glory of God motivate the Christian to evangelize?

MYTH 8

Hell Should Be Left Out of Evangelism

In an age such as ours, should we really mention hell when evangelizing? What about the damage done by people who speak only of hell or emphasize it excessively? Is there a way to evangelize without speaking about hell? Can we wait until a better time to mention hell, perhaps after the person has been going to church for a while or specifically asks about it?

In many Christian circles, there is an unspoken belief that we must tone down all mention of hell or future judgment when talking to the lost. Formally, many Christians would say they believe in hell. But when it comes to evangelism, many would say that to speak much of hell is an ineffective if not harmful approach. The phrase *fire and brimstone* is used today in a pejorative sense, even by Christians, even though two centuries ago it was a common topic of preaching, whether in church or to the lost. There is a tacit belief that preaching on hell and judgment does not work in a culture as sophisticated as ours. But

Tertullian, writing around AD 200, shows that the same ridicule and scorn regarding hell was cast on Christians in his day too: "We get ourselves laughed at for proclaiming that God will one day judge the world, though, like us, poets and philosophers set up a judgment seat in the world below. And if we threaten Gehenna, a reservoir of secret fire under the earth for purposes of punishment, we have derision heaped upon us."[1]

This implies that Christians were speaking about hell in their evangelism, regardless of the "derision heaped upon" them by the culture. Also, nowhere in the writings of the early church is there any mention of Christians advising a more soft-peddled approach to topics such as hell in order to accommodate their "sophisticated" culture. Christians are never seen arguing that people in their day are different from those in the Old Testament times and that another strategy should be advised. This goes back to the modern church's obsession for "the one" to be saved at the expense of biblical evangelism and the belief that for the one to be saved, the gospel must be presented in an attractive and inoffensive fashion.

When it comes to speaking about hell, too many Christians act like Peter when the Jews came from

---

1. Tertullian, "Apology," in *The Ante-Nicene Fathers*, ed. Alexander Roberts and James Donaldson (Peabody, Mass.: Hendrickson, 1994), 47.

Jerusalem and Paul had to rebuke him (Gal. 2:11–21). Peter acted one way with one group but differently with another. Christians have no problem admitting the realities of hell with other Christians, but when it comes to the lost, they no longer have such confidence. Many times, the Christian will take the side of the lost, believing it a shameful thing for hell to be mentioned in so plain and bold a manner. Many believe hell should be silenced altogether until "the right time." But when did talking to the lost about hell become so taboo? When did Christians become so ashamed of hell?

John MacArthur gives some alarming examples of this. He agrees that "God's wrath is almost entirely missing from modern presentations of the gospel. It is not fashionable to speak of God's wrath against sin or to tell people they should fear God."[2] Elsewhere he says, "The typical presentation today starts exactly opposite where Paul started. He wrote of 'the wrath of God...against all ungodliness and unrighteousness of men.' But modern evangelism begins with, 'God loves you and wants to make you happy.'"[3] MacArthur even likens evangelism that deliberately removes any mention of hell or the wrath of God to heresy: "Rather than arousing fear of God,

---

2. John MacArthur, *Ashamed of the Gospel* (Wheaton, Ill.: Crossway, 1993), 143.

3. MacArthur, *Ashamed of the Gospel*, 143.

it attempts to portray Him as fun, jovial, easygoing, lenient, and even permissive. Haughty sinners who ought to approach God in terror (cf. Luke 18:13) are emboldened to presume on His grace. Sinners hear nothing of divine wrath. That is as wrong as preaching rank heresy."[4] MacArthur notes that downplaying God's wrath or hell "does not enhance evangelism; it undermines it."[5] He then provides sobering statistics from a survey given to seminary students in 1992, and we can assume the numbers would be even more troubling today: "Nearly half—46 percent—feel that preaching about hell to unbelievers is in 'poor taste.'"[6] Just as disappointing were some quotations pulled from "user-friendly churches," which describes their method of preaching. Each line represents a different church and has been extracted from a larger block of description in order to point out the specific reference to hell:

1. There is no fire and brimstone here.

2. You won't hear people threatened with hell or referred to as sinners.

3. No ranting, no raving. No fire and brimstone. He doesn't even use the H-word.

4. MacArthur, *Ashamed of the Gospel*, 75.

5. MacArthur, *Ashamed of the Gospel*, 77.

6. MacArthur, *Ashamed of the Gospel*, 77.

4. You won't hear a lot of preaching about sin and damnation and hell fire.

5. It's a salvationist message, but the idea is not so much being saved from the fires of hell.[7]

It would be dishonest to say this problem never plagues Reformed churches or their approach to evangelism. Although Reformed churches may approach the doctrine of hell in a more biblical way, in general they are just as hesitant to speak about the "H-word" to the lost. In their attempt to reach the world, they have toned down the realities of hell, and in doing so they have abandoned their apparent allegiance to the doctrines of grace and Reformed Christianity. Some Christians omit speaking about hell for the sake of winning "the one" to Christ, but in doing so they actually hurt their witness:

> No sincere Christian intends to deceive sinners. In love for souls, true evangelicals invariably present some profound truths in their witnessing. Yet by the unconscious omission of essential ingredients of the Gospel, many fail to communicate even that portion of God's Word which they mean to convey. When a half truth is presented as the whole truth, it becomes an untruth.[8]

---

7. MacArthur, *Ashamed of the Gospel*, 59.

8. Walter J. Chantry, *Today's Gospel* (Edinburgh: Banner of Truth, 1970), 17.

When it comes to evangelism, hell must be spoken of, especially considering the Bible's constant allusion to its reality and danger. Our love for God and for man should drive us to speak about it, regardless of how distasteful it is to both our pagan and Christian cultures. Paul himself speaks of divine wrath as one of the primary reasons for evangelism: "Knowing therefore the terror of the Lord, we persuade men" (2 Cor. 5:11). Jesus spoke about hell more than any other person in the Bible, including the Old Testament prophets. He warned us to "fear him, which after he hath killed hath power to cast into hell" (Luke 12:5). John, the apostle of love, tells us, "And whosoever was not found written in the book of life was cast into the lake of fire" (Rev. 20:15). If these men were not ashamed to speak of hell, we should not be either.

Will Metzger notices that "our inclination to downplay the existence of hell reflects the tendency we have to compromise the gospel. I used to avoid mentioning hell. I didn't want to frighten people. I was aware that people could be manipulated and seek salvation merely as a 'fire escape.'"[9] He apparently got over it, saying, "Part of telling the truth is reinforcing the reality and danger of hell, of which the Bible speaks clearly."[10]

9. Metzger, *Tell the Truth*, 96.
10. Metzger, *Tell the Truth*, 96.

We must speak of hell because it demonstrates the justice of God. Hell reveals that God is a sin-avenging judge, not the apathetic grandpa of contemporary evangelicalism. Jesus used the most horrid descriptions imaginable when it came to hell. Language fails to describe what omnipotent wrath will accomplish against the sinner in hell, yet we must do our best to communicate its realities. Rather than knocking our heads over the question about whether God could actually govern such a place as hell, it is time to take God's Word for what it is—a revelation from the God who cannot lie (Titus 1:2)—and take such a message (the hard stuff too) to those who are perishing.

It is contradictory for persons to be saved from hell and yet, over time, to become apathetic when it comes to trying to save others from hell themselves: "Many of us who have entered the kingdom have come perilously close to the flames of the pit. We have felt its fire, and yet we have, perhaps, forgotten that from which we have been delivered."[11] Later on Jeremy Walker asks, "If hell is the least part of what it is presented to be in God's holy Word, through those Spirit-inspired Scriptures, then how in the name and for the sake of our own humanity, let alone our Christian duty, could we ever remain silent about the

---

11. Jeremy Walker, *The Brokenhearted Evangelist* (Grand Rapids: Reformation Heritage Books, 2012), x.

truth that saves from hell?"[12] If we believe it, we are dutybound to share it. If we don't believe it, we are making God out to be a liar and are ourselves in danger of the wrath to come. There are no other options.

Reflection Questions

1. Why are Christians hesitant to mention hell when evangelizing? Have you experienced this in your own evangelism?

2. As Christians, what are some ways to get over our negative stigma of hell? How can we explain hell to an unbeliever in a way that glorifies the cross?

3. Would you say most unbelievers (or even many Christians) believe hell is unfair? How would you explain the fairness of hell to people?

---

12. Walker, *Brokenhearted Evangelist*, 35.

Only Church Leaders and Professionals Should Evangelize

Should only church leaders and professionals speak to the lost about Christ since they have credentials and more experience than others? If not, who should be doing evangelism? If regular Christians evangelize, won't they be more likely to compromise the gospel or make mistakes when sharing it?

Such distinctions between clergy and laity have no bearing when it comes to evangelism. It is true some men have been gifted, qualified, and called to oversee flocks or to teach and equip others how to do the work of ministry, but Ephesians 4:8–16 shows that everyone is obligated to do the work of ministry. All Christians are priests (1 Peter 2:5), and all disciples are commanded to teach others what they know about Christ (Matt. 28:16–20). The Great Commission was not only for the disciples of Jesus's day; otherwise, they were failures. The command was to make disciples of all nations, not just the few nations they would reach in their lifetimes. As Christians, we all have the obligation to evangelize and are called to participate in the Great Commission.

Throughout church history, nonordained, "regular" Christians have often had direct influence, through the Spirit's grace, with regard to the conversion of the lost. Through sharing the gospel in their workplace, in the markets, and with their families and friends, everyday believers have been used mightily to spread the gospel evangelistically. For example, following the martyrdom of Stephen in the early church, we are told that "at that time there was a great persecution against the church which was at Jerusalem; and they were all scattered abroad throughout the regions of Judaea and Samaria, except the apostles" (Acts 8:1). The leaders of the church remained in Jerusalem. The "regular" Christians were scattered. But what did they do upon being scattered? Did they keep silent about Christ? Did they wait for the leaders to come and do the evangelism? On the contrary, we are told, "They that were scattered abroad went every where preaching the word" (v. 4). This has been the pattern, not the exception, throughout church history.

For example, the workplace has always been one of the primary places of evangelism for Christians both today and in the early church: "The chief agents in the expansion of Christianity appear not to have been those who made it a profession...but men and women who carried on their livelihood in some purely secular manner and spoke of their faith to those they met in this natural fashion."[1] This is why if we are not evangelizing at work we lose one of our primary opportunities to share the gospel with the lost. This is also why Christians shouldn't retreat into monasteries or caves.

The author is not advocating for employees to use time on the clock to evangelize. Christians at work are being paid to work, which does not give them license to steal (in the form of time). Having a good work ethic will complement any gospel witness, while having a poor work ethic will compromise it. But most jobs provide excellent evangelism opportunities during breaks, lunch, or before and after hours. We must take advantage of every opportunity we have to speak Christ unto the lost, regardless of the reaction, so long as it does not conflict with other God-given responsibilities that we have.

Another historian puts it this way: "Being excluded from the normal social gatherings, their points of contact with non-Christians lay quite inevitably at street corners or at places of employment, or in the working quarters of dwellings."[2] He even says that "evangelizing in private settings" was one of the most influential contexts for bringing about conversions

---

1. Kenneth S. Latourette, *A History of the Expansion of Christianity* (New York: Harper, 1944), 1:230.

2. Ramsay MacMullen, *Christianizing the Roman Empire* (New Haven, Conn.: Yale University Press, 1984), 40.

to the Christian religion "en masse."[3] Consider the words of Celsus, a second-century non-Christian writing about how Christians evangelized in his day:

> In private houses also we see wool-workers, cobblers, laundry-workers, and the most illiterate and bucolic yokels, who would not dare to say anything at all in front of their elders and more intelligent masters. But whenever they get hold of children in private and some stupid women with them, they let out some astounding statements as, for example, that they must not pay attention to their father and school-teacher, but must obey them instead; they say that these talk nonsense and have no understanding, and that in reality they neither know nor are able to do anything good, but are taken up with mere empty chatter. But they alone, they say, know the right way to live, and if the children would believe them, they would become happy and make their home happy as well…. But, if they like, they should leave father and their schoolmasters, and go alone with the women and little children who are their playfellows to the wooldresser's shop, or to the cobbler's or the washerwoman's shop, that they may learn perfection. And by saying this they persuade them.[4]

Most Christians in the early church reserved their evangelism "to private houses," which was "the chief

3. MacMullen, *Christianizing the Roman Empire*, 29.
4. MacMullen, *Christianizing the Roman Empire*, 37.

locus of conversion."[5] There were few missionaries. In fact, missionaries are rarely mentioned at all after the New Testament record. Christians by necessity had to keep a low profile. This does not mean evangelism wasn't being done. It is clear from the church's growth that widespread evangelism was taking place. It just shows how important every Christian is to the work of evangelism, whether or not they are ordained ministers, and how often God uses such people to add to His church. But such persons will still face persecution if they are faithful to evangelize in a biblical way: "Persecution, then, is not incidental to prophesying [preaching] but an ordained element of the prophet's life. And he who witnesses for Christ and His evangel is a prophet. If he truly loves Christ, as he must, persecution will not deter him from witnessing."[6]

If the Christian refuses to share the gospel in such spheres and with such people, who will do it? The Mormons? The Roman Catholics? The fact that Christians are not called to leave the world for a monastery or desert should be a reminder that one of our purposes in the world is to evangelize the lost in accordance with the God-decreed schedules and relationships we have.

---

5. MacMullen, *Christianizing the Roman Empire*, 111.
6. Workman, *Persecution in the Early Church*, 104.

Although planned or intentional evangelism is great, the reality is that Christians have a host of daily evangelism opportunities. What is difficult is the inevitable confrontation evangelism causes, especially with the people we know. But we are still called to do it, remembering that Jesus has all authority in heaven and earth, so we must "go, therefore." We must speak about Christ to those contacts He has given us, using the gospel and intercessory prayer as our primary instruments. We are a peculiar people, after all, and must be ready and even eager to meet a storm of hatred at any time.

To know every Christian should be evangelizing can cause disturbance and shame for many Christians. Most of us feel inadequate when it comes to sharing the gospel. But consider the demoniac, who was told right after his conversion to go and tell all about what Jesus had done for him (Mark 5:19). He knew enough of the gospel to share it with others. Rather than being afraid to do it, his overwhelming love for Christ drove him on.

That is precisely why new Christians are often the most passionate evangelists. Without any training or encouragement whatsoever, they can be amazingly effective in bringing others to Christ. They are not obsessed with technique or stymied by fear of rejection. The sheer, grand glory of the gospel fills their hearts and their vision, and they want to talk to everyone about it.[7]

Evangelism is pointing people to Christ, and if a person has been saved, they know enough about Christ to talk about Him with others. "In the sphere to which God has appointed you (in consideration of your calling, circumstances, gifts, and graces), are you prepared to speak a word for Jesus Christ? If you are not, it is sin. It is sin to keep silent when those around us are dying."[8] John MacArthur's congregation provides an example remarkably similar to the evangelism scene in the early church, and it is one that all of our churches should strive to emulate: "People in our church witness to their neighbors, coworkers, other parents in Little League, friends at school, people in the markets, their doctors, their attorneys, and everyone they meet. And over the years the Lord has blessed that one-to-one evangelistic activity to bring more people to faith in Christ than any service, program, or event we sponsor."[9]

This is why not only church leaders should speak to the lost about Christ, as demonstrated by Paul telling Timothy to "do the work of an evangelist" (2 Tim. 4:5), but everyone who is a disciple of Christ.

---

7. MacArthur and Johnson, "Rediscovering Biblical Evangelism," v.

8. Walker, *Brokenhearted Evangelist*, 33.

9. MacArthur, *Ashamed of the Gospel*, 194.

Credentials, experience, piety, and a knowledge of the Bible, though useful, are by no means the qualification for evangelism. All Christians are qualified since all Christians know the Savior. All Christians must be about the business of evangelism, trusting in the Holy Spirit to give them wisdom and words to speak.

Reflection Questions

1. How many people do you know who have been saved through a coworker's witness? How many through a friend's witness? Would you say this is the norm?

2. Do you think evangelizing at work is a good idea? Why or why not?

3. Are you surprised that evangelizing at work has been a common practice among Christians since the early church?

The Church Is Unimportant for Evangelism

Is the church important when it comes to evangelism? Is the church really necessary, considering each believer has the Holy Spirit and the Bible? Is evangelism concerned only about speaking Christ to the lost, regardless of church or where believers gather?

The church is probably not going to be the first item brought up when we evangelize. Also, making a plug or recommendation for your church is not to be equated with evangelism, even though there is nothing wrong with this. That being said, it should be emphasized that the way God raises up His kingdom on earth is through converted men and women joining together in fellowship "for the gathering and perfecting of the saints,"[1] which takes place because evangelism has happened to them at some point. The way God equips His people to be better at doing evangelism is through His church, specifically the

---

1. Westminster Confession of Faith 25.3.

evangelists, pastors, and teachers He has called in part for this purpose (Eph. 4:8–16). This is why the model of personal evangelism exhibited by pastors and teachers is so important, as well as intentional sermons, teachings, or trainings that help the flock better share the gospel.

When Paul went to a certain place to evangelize, the Lord typically blessed the effort with converts. Paul's task was then to meet with the converts, teaching them and assigning elders to oversee them. These new converts and elders then continued to do the work of evangelism, bringing converts into their local fellowship where they, too, would be taught and equipped for the work of ministry. This has been the process throughout church history, and it is the same today.

The apostle Paul is an excellent example. The churches in Acts were filled with "many signs and wonders" (Acts 5:12). Because of this, there was a tendency among the unbelieving people to keep away from the church: "And of the rest durst no man join himself to them" (v. 13). When Paul was converted, however, he immediately sought to be "with the disciples which were at Damascus" (Acts 9:19). He did not stay away from the church. When he went to Jerusalem shortly afterward, far from being nomadic or a lone wolf, "he assayed to join himself to the disciples" (v. 26). This was the pattern of Paul's life and ministry, and it should be the same for every Christian.

Evangelism without attachment to the local church is unhealthy and potentially dangerous, especially if it leads to conversions. The newly converted are the most prone to fall into heretical camps. They are hungry for the Word, so they go to whatever gathering they have heard about, usually without much knowledge of biblical churches. Assuming they are truly converted, they may spend years bouncing around looking for a healthy church before they come to a better understanding of what a true church is. Such a scenario is grievous.

In the Great Commission passage, Jesus tells the disciples to teach others "to observe all things whatsoever I have commanded you" (Matt. 28:20). It is no accident that wherever the church has spread, one of its first tasks has typically been to set up centers of learning, especially of reading. The church in part is responsible for teaching the converted about Christ's life and message, which is found in the Scriptures. The church is called to help believers to be learners of Christ and, just as importantly, to be imitators of Christ.

In this same passage, Christ speaks of baptism, which is an ordinance done through the church. This is an important aspect of evangelism. If you were to look at the various kinds of churches and worship services throughout history, the distinctions would be dizzying. The church in Acts would have done things differently from a church in the contemporary

West or even when compared to churches in the time of Augustine or Calvin. Today we see churches in Africa, China, and India that have little similarity with churches in America and England. So what unites all of these groups? Aside from Scripture and certain doctrinal truths, the answer would be the sacraments—the Lord's Supper and baptism.

The Reformers held that a proper view of the sacraments was one of the ways to distinguish a true church from a false church. Baptism's importance is seen in the beginning pages of the Gospels, where Jesus Himself is baptized. Baptism communicates union with Christ and union with His body, which is the church. It demonstrates our regeneration by the Holy Spirit and the washing away of sin. This is why Christ was so adamant about baptism being done as part of the discipling process. On the day of Pentecost in Acts 2, we also see baptism as a gateway into the church. But the sacraments are something that take place within the local community of believers, not outside of it. This is why it is so important for evangelism to be done within the context of a local church. In this way, new converts will have a place where they can be baptized, partake of the Lord's Supper, and be discipled.

It is easy for the Christian to have a nomadic mindset because of criticism, disagreement, or lack of support from within the church. He may become discouraged or even embittered as a result. But the local church is Christ's bride and should be cherished accordingly. When it comes to evangelism, everyone has blind spots or questions. When Paul was doing ministry in strange lands, he always reverted to the Jerusalem Council whenever a difficult question came up. What is more, he always submitted to its decision. He also returned regularly to Antioch, his sending church, and was in constant communication with the churches and the collaborators within the communities where he evangelized.

The local church is extremely important for evangelism. It can provide insight into the workings of the Spirit, locating and suggesting areas where evangelism could be useful. It can also help by supplying tracts and prayer. Even if the church lacks financial support, it should not lack people who pray for such an important task. The church should also be a place of encouragement for the one who is evangelizing. Especially in our day, evangelizing can be disappointing. The West is not seeing many converts. Christians who evangelize in the West are beginning to experience real persecution. Being in the midst of other believers who are going through similar trials can be advantageous spiritually and encourage us not to quit.

The church is a place where believers worship the Lord, partake in the sacraments, and are equipped for the work of ministry (which includes evangelism) through the preaching and teaching of the Word. But Christ's church is to be spread throughout the world, as we see in the Great Commission, and this is done not only through regular evangelistic preaching in the church but also through the local church sending out missionaries, evangelists, and everyday Christians who bring the gospel to the lost. This is why the church is so important when it comes to evangelism.

Reflection Questions

1. How are believers equipped to evangelize through their local church?

2. What are some dangers of evangelizing without having a local church to either equip you or send disciples or converts to?

3. How can you explain the importance of the local church with Christians who don't want to go to church or who don't have a local church they are part of?

Conclusion

How would Christians in the West respond if it suddenly became illegal to meet together for church or study the Scriptures or attend prayer meetings? Would we do so anyway? Or would we stop meeting together, knowing that if we did meet, our freedom or perhaps our bank accounts could be compromised? Perhaps our family would be put at risk. Perhaps we could lose our lives.

This scenario is not exactly hypothetical. Such a day is likely on the horizon in the West, as demonstrated during the COVID-19 pandemic. But when it comes to evangelism, things are much different. It is possible to meet in secret when it comes to worship and Bible studies, without society knowing about it. But evangelism necessarily involves the unbelieving community knowing what we believe, including the offensive parts, since it is the unbelieving persons of society we are called to evangelize. Evangelism requires the Christian to confront the worldview of an unbelieving person with the truth of the gospel, which is why the one evangelizing will be the first to see persecution and retaliation from society. We are commanded to evangelize. We do not have the luxury of simply stopping the work when it becomes illegal or uncomfortable. Not to mention that if we desire society to change or become more lenient toward Christians, what else but conversions will make this happen? And how will people be converted unless someone is speaking to them about Christ?

When it comes to evangelism, many modern methods are unbiblical. So what do we do about it? Where do we go from here? Regardless of what sphere the Lord has called us to as Christians, we have an opportunity to evangelize the lost and help minister to others. When it comes to evangelizing the lost, we must stick to biblical methods alone, which are actually quite simple, as we have seen—gospel proclamation and intercessory prayer. We must trust God will be faithful to His Word. We must trust that God's wisdom about how to do evangelism is superior to ours. When it comes to ministering to other Christians as it relates to evangelism, we can pray for each other. We can stir each other up and hold each other accountable to evangelize. We can encourage each other to do things biblically whenever we do evangelize.

It is more than likely many evangelizing Christians, though well-meaning, have simply never been challenged to consider what the Bible teaches about evangelism. It is easy to simply do what others have done before us, even though unbiblical. The best thing we can do for fellow believers is to patiently encourage them to think through what God's Word says about the myths addressed in this book and then help them apply biblical principles to their own evangelism.

We must remember if we ourselves are no longer using unbiblical means to evangelize the lost, it is by God's grace alone. We must speak to other believers about these issues in a way that is patient and humble, taking heed lest we fall (1 Cor. 10:12). We must genuinely desire that they grow in knowledge of God's will on such an important topic as evangelism. We must guard against coming across as harsh or proud. In doing so, it is likely our Christian brothers and sisters will reform their course in a more biblical direction.

Many myths are not addressed in this book, and many more will likely crop up in the Christian community. This is why we must constantly return to God's Word as our only infallible rule of faith and practice, having as our aim the glory of God alone—not big churches, popularity, or staying clear from persecution. As encouraging as it is to see a revival of sorts regarding Reformed theology, it is time it extends into our evangelism as well.

Lastly, not every evangelism encounter will be easy. Most of the time our flesh will rebel. We will find excuses not to do it. We will find ways to go about it that will protect us from being hated by the world or make us look more attractive to the lost. We must tenaciously strive against this. Such thinking must be pulverized. Like Paul, even though we may fear and tremble, we must pray for open doors, boldness, and more laborers to enter the harvest. We must not tamper with God's prescribed way of doing evangelism, regardless of how difficult it may seem. We must press on, remembering John Owen's bleak but astute reminder that "no people in the world need help like those who lack the gospel; for of all distresses, lack of the gospel cries the loudest for relief."

Let us go to the lost with the gospel alone, relying on Christ alone for the victory, and with the Scriptures alone as our guide. Evangelism began with God speaking to Adam in the garden. What a privilege to think God now uses weak and fearful men to cry out to others, "Believe on the Lord Jesus Christ, and thou shalt be saved, and thy house" (Acts 16:31). May we never pass up such an opportunity to speak about Christ to the lost. May we go and imitate the Master, remembering "the harvest truly is plenteous, but the labourers are few" (Matt. 9:37).